Gentle German Shepherds

A COLOURING BOOK FOR ADULTS

Paws for Thought: Vol. 4

Christine Vencato

This book is dedicated to my wonderful family

Illustrations and design © 2016 Christine Vencato

www.arttherapycolouringbook.org

First edition; first printing

All rights reserved. No part of this book may be reproduced or copied except for your own personal, home use - limited to simple reproduction through photocopy and scan/print. You may not scan into electronic form for the purpose of distribution without the express permission from the copyright holder.

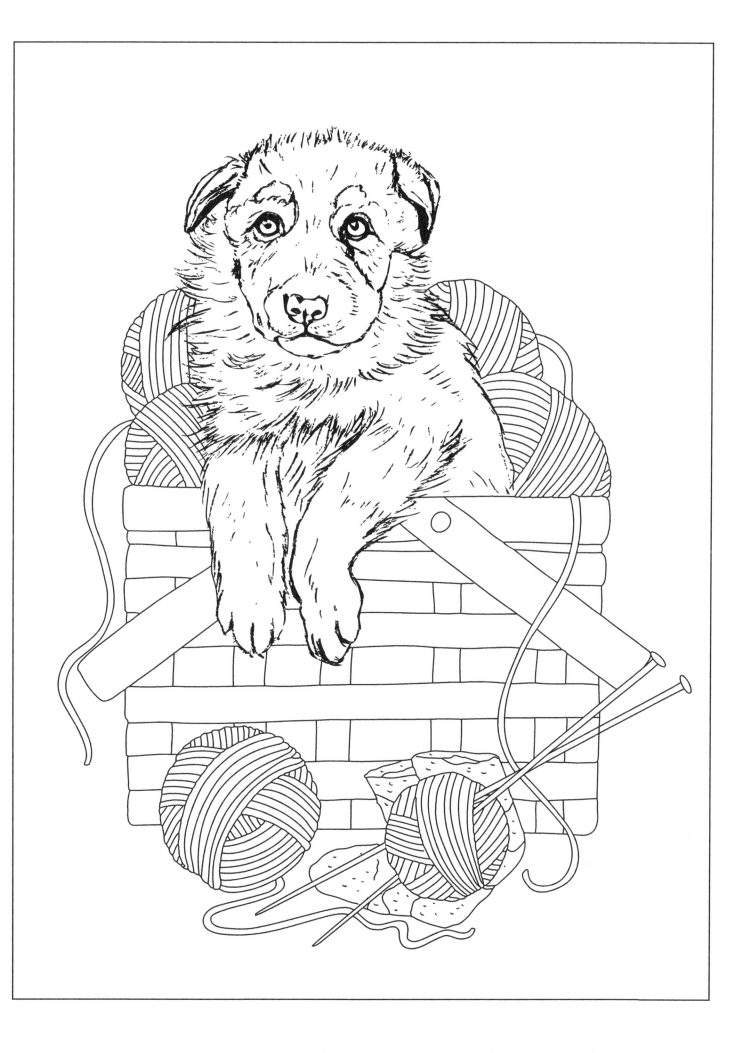

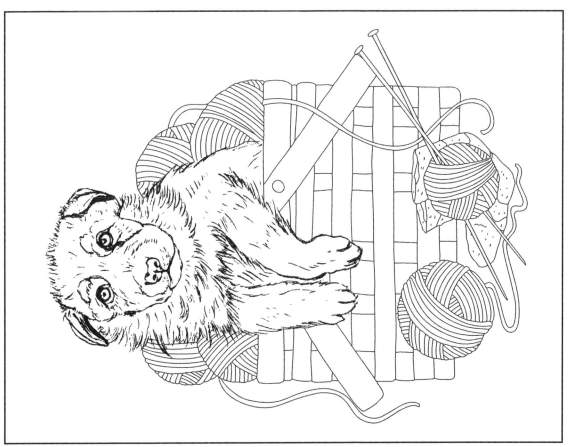

PLEASE VISIT WWW.ARTTHERAPYCOLOURINGBOOK.ORG FOR MORE INFORMATION AND FREE COLOURING PAGES. YOU MAY ALSO BE INTERESTED IN OTHER BOOKS FROM THE SAME AUTHOR:

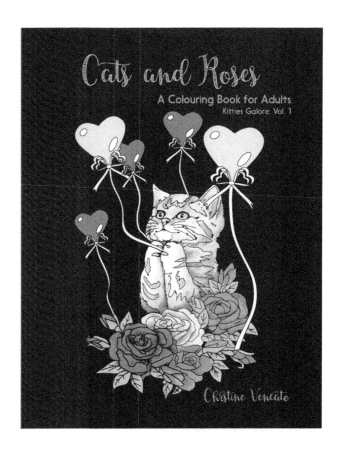

Made in the USA
Coppell, TX
13 December 2020